101 HAMBURGER JOKES

...meaty jokes to be devoured with relish

by PHIL HIRSCH

illustrated by Don Orehek

SCHOLASTIC INC.
New York Toronto London Auckland Sydney

DEDICATED
to
Barbara and Morton Held
who prefer
the tuna

ISBN 0-590-40374-5

Copyright © 1978 by Phil Hirsch. All rights reserved. Published by Scholastic Inc.

12 11 10 9 8 7 6 5 4 3 2 1   6 7 8 9/8 0/9

Printed in the U.S.A.   06

101
HAMBURGER
JOKES

simply sizzles with hilarious hamburger humor! Be the first on line to be served up a really rare joke treat— and get ready to roll with laughter at these riotous rib-ticklers!

What is the hamburgers' most
familiar song?

"Home on the Range"!

When do hamburgers most enjoy watching TV?

During prime time!

How do you make a hamburger green?

Find a yellow cheeseburger and mix it with a blue one!

The hamburger was invented in
_____.

a. *Hamburg, Germany*
b. *Burg, Tennessee*
c. *Hamlet, Ohio*
d. *Meatsico*
e. *All of the above*

Can you name two burgers who are royalty?

Sir Loin and Burger King!

What did the hamburger say when it found out that most people liked hamburgers better than frankfurters?

"Hot dog!"

Why does Farrah Fawcett-Majors
love hamburgers?

*Who knows — but we just wanted to
mention her name!*

What baseball team do the meat patties root for?

The New York Meats!

What did the hamburgers say to the butcher who acted on a TV show?

"Welcome back, Cutter!"

Which type of comedy leaves a hamburger cold?

Biting humor!

Is there a way to make a hamburger do the Hula?

Sure, order a burger and a shake!

How do you insult a hamburger patty?

Call it a meatball!

Which meatballs get a little tipsy on occasion?

The potted ones!

Why do the hamburgers beat the hot dogs at every sport they play?

Because hot dogs are the wurst!

How does a burger acquire good taste?

With a little seasoning!

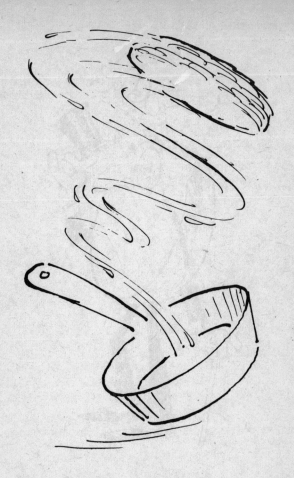

How are UFO's related to
hamburgers?

*Both are Unidentified Frying
Objects!*

Which baseball team is currently the favorite with hamburger fans?

The Cincinnati Reds — because they're the Big Bread Machine!

How do we know hamburgers have high IQ's?

They "loin" fast!

Which is the meat patties' least favorite day of the week?

Fry-day!

Where can a burger get a great
night's sleep?

On a bed of lettuce!

MOTHER

Who wins most of the medals for bravery in Burger Land?

The meatball heros!

Who can beat any burger at golf?

Any links sausage!

Are hamburgers male?

Yes, because they're boygers, not girlgers!

What is this a drawing of?

1. *a balloon flying in the wind*
2. *a Frisbee hamburger*
3. *a clam closed for the summer*
4. *a clamburger*
5. *a bionic pancake*
6. *a football stadium with the seats removed*

Answer: *Actually, it's a pet hamburger. See the leash!*

Which burger has four legs,
whiskers, and a tail?

A cat-burger! (burglar)

Can you use the word "tenderloin" in a sentence?

Burgers "tenderloin" faster than pizzas or hot dogs!

Which cheeseburger makes a big hit in baseball?

A double!

Who is the hamburgers' favorite singer?

"Hammy" Davis Jr.!

Is it proper to eat a hamburger with your fingers?

No, you should eat your fingers separately!

Seriously, is it proper to eat a hamburger with your fingers?

Not if they are lady fingers, which are best eaten with tea or milk!

What great song is associated with hamburgers and baseball?

"Steak Me Out to the Ballgame"!

Can a hamburger marry a hot dog?

Only if they have a very frank relationship!

Meaty Television Shows
— Prime Time Only!

Meaty Mouse

Meat the Press

The Lucille Meat-Ball Show

My Three Buns

I Love Juicy

Gristley Adams

Hee Hawsemeat

The Carol Burn-it Show

Kojak in the Box

Big Blue Marbled Meat

Char-lie's Angels

The Brady Bun

Where do the burgers go on New Year's Eve?

To a meat ball!

Which burgers love to act?

Ham-burgers!

Why do burgers run the gauntlet?

To test their meattle!

When the crooked hamburger took it on the "lamb," where did it go?

Oh, "ewe" know!

Seriously, when the crooked hamburger took it on the lam, where did it go?

Heidelburg-er, Germany!

What is the hamburgers' motto?

If at first you don't succeed, fry, fry again!

What happened to the pilot who flew into a 4,000-pound mountain of meat?

He got grounded!

How was the hamburger murdered?

First it was "rolled," then smothered in onions!

What do they say about the noise at
the Burger Land Super Bowl?

It's <u>pan</u>-demonium!

Which burgers can tell your fortune?

Medium burgers!

Who are the hamburgers' favorite
people?

Vegetarians!

Meaty Hamburger Proverbs

The moo the merrier.

There's no place like homeburger.

Calf a love is better than none.

Them's biting words!

You can't make a silk purse
 out of a cow's ear.

Where there's a grill there's a way.

If you can't stand the meat, get out
 of the kitchen!

Calf and the world calfs with you,
 fry and you fry alone.

How do they prevent crime in hamburger country?

With burger alarms!

How do we know burgers love young people?

They're pro-teen!

How can you tell which Burger Land baseball pitchers are left-handed?

They're the ones wearing the left-handed "meats"!

Which burger is famous for a long nose?

Cyrano de Burgerac!

What can you say about the 6'5″ chunk of meat who went into boxing?

The burger they are, the harder they fall!

What do they call a meeting among the most brilliant people in Burger Land?

A <u>meating</u> of the minds!

Why aren't burgers the least bit scared of Halloween?

They're used to people "goblin" them!

Why do hamburgers act brilliantly on stage?

They give meaty performances— especially if they are in their prime!

Who can you always rely on in Burger Land during an emergency?

Hamburger helpers!

Who do the hamburgers love on TV?

Archie Bunker's son-in-law, the meathead!

What do you use to determine if a refrigerated burger is cold enough?

A thermomeater!

What can you say about Ham Burger and Chief Justice Warren Burger?

Ham Burger is "well done," and Chief Justice Burger has "done well"!

What kind of girl does a hamburger like?

Any girl named Patty!

Meaty Movies

...each one deserves an Oscar—an Oscar Meyer!

A Star Is Bun

My Rare Lady

Burn Free

The Buns of Navarone

The French Fried Connection

The Blue Macs

Bunji

How do we know that hamburgers love classical music?

They're often found at the Meatropolitan Opera House and Cownegie Hall!

How do you make a meat loaf?

Send it on a vacation!

Which dances do the burgers do best?

The burger-loo and the char char!

Which of our meaty friends are into astrology?

Those that are born under the sign of the Ham!

In what school subjects does the teacher say, "Well done, hamburgers"?

A wide range of subjects—meatyeval history, meatematics, and word grill.

What kind of baseball do burgers play?

"Ketchup baseball!"

Why did Henry Winkler, who started the first drive-in fast-food operation, have to shut down?

He ran out of Funz!

Whom do the meat patties dislike most?

The butchers!—they're always talking chop!

Why do hamburgers make poor stool pigeons?

They won't talk no matter how long you grill them!

How far do burgers go in school?

Through cowlege (then they get their 450 degrees!).

Hamburger Hall of Flame

Walter Kronkheight

Famed newsman Walter Kronkheight devours 17 hamburgers a day wrapped up in sections of such newspapers as *The New York Times, Chicago Tribune, Washington Post,* etc. Says Kronkheight, "This makes it easy for me to digest the news!"

Parker Plotz

Sculptor Parker Plotz, of Bayou, Louisiana, has made it possible for people who don't like beef to really *want* to eat it. Plotz shapes chopped beef into chickens, fish, vegetables, and candy bars . . . and this fools non-beef eaters into thinking that they are eating other foods! Plotz, amazingly, has never heard one beef from anyone.

Name two tennis stars who are
famous in the hamburger world.

*Bjorn Borger and Billie Jean-o's
Burger King!*

Who puts holes in meat patties?

Dunkin' Hamburgers!

Who is the most important person in
a European town?

The burger-meister!

Why do burgers laugh when you surround them with pickles?

Who knows — maybe they're picklish!

Which opera is about our meaty friends?

"The Barbecue of Seville"!

What did they tell the burger who enlisted in the Army?

"You've got no beef, soldier!"

What is a hamburger's favorite story?

"Hansel and Gristle"!

Rare Vampire Jokes

How many burgers do you feed a ferocious, 14-foot-tall vampire?

All it wants!

Do hamburgers make good vampires?

No, because they always find themselves in goulash situations!

Which singer's records do they play at hamburger joints in Transylvania?

Fang Sinatra's!

What's the one food that goes over almost as well as burgers in Transylvania?

Fang-furters! (Sometimes neck-wurst!)

What did the Big Mac say when the Vampire attacked him?

"You're a pain in the neck!"

Why did the vampire go crazy at Burger King?

He saw all that catsup and wanted a transfusion!

Do they really serve burgers in Transylvania?

Very rare-ly!

Where did the burgers go after their wedding?

On a bun-eymoon!

NIAGARA FALLS

What do meatballs say about
mystery stories?

"The pot thickens!"

How do gossipy hamburgers spend
their time?

They chew the fat!

What kind of company is a 24-hour
hamburger joint?

Fry-by-night!

What famous movie did the hamburger meat think of when they took it out of the freezer?

"The Fry Who Came in from the Cold"!

What do some people have against cheeseburgers?

They say, "Burgers can't be cheesey!"

Why do hamburgers make good baseball players?

They're great at the plate!

What system do they teach in Hamburger High's math courses?

The meatric system, silly!

What old-time song is the burgers'
favorite?

"Hammy"—as sung by Al Jolson!

What do burgers think when they
are surrounded by gherkins?

They think they are in a pickle!

Which poem is the meat patties'
favorite?

*"The Charge of the Light Brigade,"
for its lines that read:*

*"Heifer league, heifer league,
heifer league onward!"*

Why is President Carter important
to Hamburger Land in April?

*On the opening day of the baseball
season, he throws out the first
meatball!*

Why do hamburgers feel sad at
barbecues?

They get to meet their old flames!

What do hamburger workers say on Monday morning?

"Well, it's back to the old grind!"

What happened when the meat patty
saw the seeded roll?

*It was love at first sight — poppy (seed)
love!*

Why did the pro football player from the last-place team drop pieces of hamburger into his soup?

He wanted to know how it felt to take part in a Soup-er Bowl!

Why don't meat patties go to many movies?

It's the same old plot — boyger meets grill!

Which political discussions between the Russians and Americans keenly interest Burger Land citizens?

The SALT talks!

What is this a drawing of?

A Burger King!

What did they do to the burger who
thought he was a rooster?

Cook-a-doodle-do!

What did the hamburger say when it pleaded "not guilty"?

"I've been flamed!"

Which burgers are dishonest?

Cat-burgers! (burglars)

Which player do the meat patties root for in pro football?

Chris Hanburger of the Washington Redskins!

What song do burgers sing on the job?

"Gristle While You Work"!

Which people do the burgers hate?

The ones who are always putting the bite on them!

What did they say about the burgers who went skiing for the first time?

How the meaty have fallen!

Who is the hamburgers' favorite actress?

Candice Berger!

Why was the magician able to make 12 meat patties disappear?

Because the handburger is quicker than the eye!

What do some burger eaters have?

A Hardee appetite!

Why aren't burgers too good at basketball?

Too many turnovers!

When do burgers quit their jobs?

The day they decide to meat loaf!

How do you make a hamburger smile?

Pickle it gently!

Hamburger Hits

Meat and My Shadow

If I Had a Hammerburger

Grill of My Dreams

Fry a Little Tenderness

Cow Much Do I Love You?

You're Still the Bun

Fry Like an Eagle

At which fast food restaurant is a hamburger happiest?

Arthur Treacher's Fish and Chips!

Why were the burgers in the refrigerator embarrassed?

They saw the salad dressing!

Why are our meaty friends so willing to take whatever comes their way?

Burgers can't be choosers!

What kind of a pitch did Sandy
Koufax of the old Burger-lyn
Dodgers have?

A fastball—a sizzler!

Who is a hamburger's favorite
comedian?

Milton Broil!(Berle)

When can you count on a hamburger
in an emergency?

When the chips are down!

How does a pitcher walk a man in
Burger Land baseball?

He throws four meatballs!

How do the Rolling Stones like their
burgers?

*Plain—Rolling Stones gather no
moss-tard!*

When does a hamburger wear a look like a smile button?

When somebody says, "Well done"!

Why are hamburgers essential to football?

Because the game is played on a griddle-iron!

Who was the burger's favorite all-time movie director?

Sizzle B. DeMille!

Why was the burger thrown out of the Army?

He couldn't pass mustard! (muster)

How do you make a cheeseburger
sad?

Make it with blue cheese!

Where does a burger go on vacation?

The Swiss (cheese) Alps or The Cheeseapeake Valley!

Where is home to a burger?

Any old cow town!

Where does a burger feel at home?

On the range!

What did they call it when NHL officials refused to allow a hamburger to play hockey in the league?

Rink injustice!

Why can any hamburger run the mile in under four minutes?

Because it's a <u>fast</u> food!

What are some outstanding
hamburger colleges?

*Brandeis, Cowlifornia State,
Hoofstra, Pen State, Ranchelaer
Polytechnic, Burgereley, and
Moosouri!*

What happens when two burgers fall
in love?

*They live together in holy
meatrimony!*

How did the jury find the
hamburger?

Grill-ty as charred!

The Hamburger IQ Test)

1. The hamburger is called a "fast food" because _____.

   a. it runs the mile in under four minutes.
   b. if the onions are raw, it quickly moves you to tears.
   c. it wins every track "meat."

2. The "ham" in hamburger comes from _____.

   a. its popularity in every hamlet.
   b. Shakespeare's play, "Hamlet," because Hamlet preferred burgers to his girl, Ophelia.
   c. people making "pigs" of themselves because they can't stop eating them.

3. Hamburgers are the national dish in _____.

   a. Hamsterdam.
   b. the Bergershire Mountains.
   c. meatropolitan Los Angeles.

Note: If you answered each question, you are a real meatball! For your mis-information, the correct answer to each question is "d."